Grandma Shares
Her Faith

Cain and Abel

Grandma Shares Her Faith

Cain and Abel

Second in a Series

LAURA LIPARI

REDSCORPION
PRESS

To my children,
John, Charles, Myriam, Vivian, Tom,
with love

GRANDMA SHARES HER FAITH

Cain & Abel

Laughter and squealing could be heard from outside the house. Grandma looked out the window and saw her grandchildren racing down the street. She smiled and turned away from the window. Going into the study, she picked up the Bible. Just then the door opened with a bang. The children rushed in, breathing hard. Loren threw himself down on the carpeted floor.

"I'm exhausted!" he said. "No matter how hard I try, I can't beat Angela in a race."

"Does that bother you?"

"Yes, Grandma, it bothers me a lot. I hate to admit that a girl can beat me, especially when I'm older than she is."

Marie tried to comfort Loren. "Don't let

that upset you. She not only beats the girls in her class, but even most of the boys."

"I don't know how she does it. She's like that little bunny on TV that runs on batteries and keeps going and going and going."

"Where's Angela now?" Grandma asked.

"Running around the block. She said she wanted to finish the race," Marie answered.

"Oh, here she comes now," Jade announced.

Angela walked briskly into the room, face flushed, but breathing normally. Not so with Chompers, her trusty dog. He was panting hard. He walked slowly to Loren and plopped down beside him.

"I know exactly how you feel, pal," Loren said, patting the dog.

"Sorry for keeping you waiting, Grandma," Angela said. "Are you going to continue with the Bible story now?"

"Just as soon as you children take your places."

"Grandma, could you wait just a few minutes while I go to say hello to Gabby?"

"No, honey, let's finish our Bible story first, and then you can spend as much time as you want talking to Gabby."

"Am I glad you said no, Grandma," Marie said, "because when she and Gabby get going, you never know when they're going to stop. I just can't understand how she talks to him."

"Maybe because it's bird talk. She certainly has a way with animals," Loren remarked.

"Gabby is not an animal, dummy. He's a bird," Marie said with a look of superiority.

"Okay, so she has a way with birds too."

"Let's not waste any more time, children. Let's get started with our Bible story. Where did we leave off yesterday?"

"Where God kicked Adam and Eve out of the garden."

"Loren, can you think of a better word than 'kicked'?"

"Yes, Grandma: 'banished.' God banished them from the garden."

"That's better. Not long after Adam and Eve left the garden, a baby boy was born to them. They called him Cain. Later on, they had another baby boy and they named him Abel. Cain grew up to be a farmer and Abel was a shepherd. After the harvest—"

"Excuse me, Grandma, what's a harvest?" Desy asked.

"Loren, would you like to explain to Desy what a harvest is?"

"Yes, Grandma. It's like when our neighbors go out to the field at the end of summer with their big machines to gather up the ripe corn and potatoes, or whatever else they planted."

"Now do you understand what 'harvest' means?" Grandma asked.

Desy nodded.

Grandma continued: "Cain took some of his harvest and offered it to God. It was his way of thanking God. And Abel

offered God his firstborn lamb. God was pleased with Abel's gift but not with Cain's."

"Why wasn't God pleased with Cain's gift?" Jade asked.

"Maybe He didn't like the corn," Desy suggested.

"Is that what Cain offered God? Corn?" Angela asked.

"We don't know exactly what Cain offered. It could have been wheat, barley, or something else."

"But God did like the lamb. I'm sure God liked it better than any vegetable that Cain brought Him," Angela said with a knowing smile.

"It could have been fruit, couldn't it?" Jade asked.

"The lamb would still be better than fruit. At least you can play a long time with a cute, fuzzy, little lamb."

"Because you are such an animal lover, Angela, I can see why you would think that God would prefer the lamb to vegetables, fruit, or anything else," Grandma told her. "However, I feel nothing Cain might have offered God would have been acceptable to Him."

"Even if he had offered a lamb?"

"Even if Cain had offered God a lamb, God would not have accepted it."

"But God accepted a lamb from Abel. Why wouldn't He accept one from Cain?" a puzzled Angela asked.

"God would not have accepted the lamb, or anything else that Cain might have offered Him."

"Why, Grandma?" Jade was confused.

"Because Cain's behavior was not pleasing to God."

"What did he do?" the children wanted to know.

"The Bible doesn't explain what Cain did to displease God. But because we know that God is very patient and doesn't get angry quickly or easily, we must come to the conclusion that God had a good reason to be angry with Cain. When Cain saw that God accepted Abel's gift but not his, he became upset and his face showed how angry he was. God saw the frown on Cain's forehead and asked, 'Why are you frowning? If you had done the right thing, you would be smiling instead of frowning. And sin is trying to get the best of you. But don't let sin control you. You can still make things right.'"

"Oh, I get it, Grandma," Loren said. "Cain must have done something wrong, because God said to him, 'If you had done the right thing . . .'"

"I agree with Loren," Marie interrupted. "Even though the Bible doesn't tell us exactly what Cain did, I think Cain did something wrong."

"Grandma," Loren whispered with a twinkle in his eye, "what a miracle! Marie actually agrees with me!"

Grandma smiled. "God wanted to help

Cain and assured him, 'You are still in time to make things right.' You see, God loved Cain as much as He loved Abel."

"And of course, Cain did what God told him to do," Jade said.

"No, he didn't, but he should have. One day, Cain invited his brother to go out into the fields with him. I'm sure Abel was very happy that Cain asked him to go with him. When they reached the fields, do you know what happened? Without a warning, Cain killed his brother."

"Killed his brother! Why?" The children were shocked.

"He was jealous of his brother. He was still angry that God had accepted Abel's gift and not his. In his jealousy and anger, he thought it was Abel's fault that God had refused his gift, and he was going to make Abel pay for it. All he could think of was how to get even with Abel."

"What an awful thing to do just because he was jealous," Loren commented.

"Many times when people are angry, they don't think clearly, and instead of fixing things, they make matters worse. Rather than blaming Abel, Cain should have asked God why He had refused his gift."

"Grandma, how come Cain turned out to be a bad guy? You said God was happy because everything He created was very good. Yesterday we learned about a bad snake, and now about a bad person. Since everything was good, how come Cain was bad?" Jade was puzzled.

"That's a good question. Many have asked that same question over the years and continue to do so even today. I'll try my best to answer it. When God made us, he gave us free will—the ability to make choices and decisions. He didn't make us like puppets whose every move is controlled. Would you like to have someone to tell you all the time what to do, how to do it, and when to do it? God didn't want us to be like wooden marionettes on a string. Would you like to live all your life like a puppet with someone pulling your strings?"

They all shook their heads, and Marie declared, "No one is going to pull my strings!"

"I'm glad you feel that way. It's good to be able to make our own decisions. And we should use God's gift wisely in deciding which road to take in life. Cain chose the wrong way, and Abel chose the right way. And because of Cain another sin entered the world. Can anyone tell me what that sin was?"

"Killing his brother!" Marie shouted.

"Murder," Loren added.

"You're both right. What was the first sin?"

"Disobedience," the children answered.

"When did sin enter the world?"

"After Eve ate the forbidden fruit," Loren answered promptly.

"Don't forget, Adam took a bite of the

fruit too," Marie hastened to add.

"So, they were the first sinners?"

"You're wrong, Loren," Marie objected. "They weren't the first to sin."

"They weren't? Who else could have sinned first? If Eve didn't, who did?"

"Lucifer."

"Lucifer? Who's he?" Loren was curious.

"He was a good angel once, but now he's a bad one."

"Are you making this up? How can an angel be bad?" Loren looked at Marie suspiciously.

"An angel can be bad. And for your information, Loren, I'm not making this up. It's true! Lucifer is a bad angel."

"But Grandma, I always thought that angels are good, and that's why they're called angels. I just can't agree with Marie.

Angels can't be bad," Jade insisted.

"I think we should give Marie a chance to explain about Lucifer!" And turning to Marie, Grandma said encouragingly, "Marie, we are all interested in hearing about the bad angel."

"How come you know about this bad angel?" Jade gave Marie a doubtful look.

"I do go to Sunday school, you know," Marie announced, rolling her eyes with impatience. "My Sunday school teacher told us about him. You wanna hear what she told us?"

Yes, the children were very much interested in knowing about this angel and eager for her to begin. They almost lost their patience as they waited for Marie, who was busy straightening out her shoulders, sitting up taller, trying to look like a teacher, and looking around to be sure she had everyone's attention before beginning.

Then, with a toss of her head, she said, "One day our teacher asked us if we knew about Lucifer. None of us did, so she explained that God created all the angels. They were all beautiful and very good. But Lucifer, whose name means 'light,' was the most beautiful and important of all the angels. Lucifer became jealous of God. He wanted to *be* God. So he got a bunch of angels to fight with him against God. The dummy was sure he could be God. But God quickly showed Lucifer and his good-for-nothing angel friends who was boss. And God punished Lucifer and his stupid angels by kicking—I mean *throwing* them out of Heaven and making them fall way, way down into Hell. And that's when the first sin was committed."

"Very good, Marie," praised Grandma.

Marie smiled with pride.

"Marie, was he the one who made Eve eat the apple?" asked Desy.

"It wasn't an apple. Remember?" said Marie.

"Oh yeah. I forgot for a moment. Well, whatever fruit it was."

"I'm not sure, Desy, if he was the one who fooled Eve, but if he wasn't the one, it could have been one of his devil buddies."

"But now let's get back to Cain's sin," Grandma said in an effort to guide them back to the story.

"After Cain killed his brother, did God kill Cain?" Angela asked.

"No, he didn't."

"He *didn't*? He deserved to die for killing his brother. And I bet God was awfully mad at Cain," Jade said.

"I think He was more pained and dis-appointed than angry," Grandma re-marked.

"When did God find out that Cain killed his brother?"

"God knew right away, because He's omniscient."

"He's what?" Angela asked.

"He's omniscient."

"And what does that mean?" Angela asked.

"It means God knows everything," Loren replied.

"That's right, Loren," Grandma said. "God knew, but He wanted Cain to tell Him. So God called Cain and asked where Abel was. You know what Cain replied?"

"I bet Cain told God he didn't know," Marie answered.

"Right. He lied. And then he asked

God sarcastically, 'Am I my brother's keeper?'"

"Grandma, what does that mean?" Desy asked.

"Cain was saying, 'Am I responsible for my brother? Do I have to take care of him? Just because I'm older than he is, do I have to look after him?' Children, let's stop for a moment and consider that question. Just suppose we were to ask God, 'Am I my brother's keeper?' What do you think God would answer?" Grandma asked.

"I think He would say yes, because He would want me to look after my brother," Loren said.

"No, He wouldn't, Loren, because you don't have a brother," Jade told him.

"Jade, you're missing the point," Grandma said. "God is telling all of us that we must take care of one another—family, friends, neighbors, and those who need help, regardless of the color of their skin, their religion, or their nationality. We are all descendants of Adam and Eve; we are all God's children. Now do you understand why we are 'our brother's keeper'?"

The children nodded.

"Now, back to Cain—"

"But Grandma," Jade interrupted, "did God finally make Cain die for what he did?"

"No, Jade, God didn't make Cain die. But since God is a just God, He had to punish Cain for doing such a wicked thing."

"Did God put Cain in jail?" Angela asked.

"No, there were no jails in those days. They didn't need them. But since God had spilled his brother's blood on the ground, God said the soil would no longer grow anything that Cain planted."

"Then he couldn't be a farmer anymore and grow his own food?" Angela asked.

"That's right. God also told Cain that he would be a restless man, moving all the time, never staying long in one place."

"Just like a hobo," Loren suggested.

"That's a good comparison. Cain was very frightened. He cried out to God that such a harsh punishment was more than he could take, and he was afraid that anyone who saw him would kill him."

"And did someone kill him?" Desy asked.

"Luckily for Cain, no."

"So, then did God let him go free?" the disappointed children asked.

"Oh, no. God didn't let Cain go free,

but why didn't God make him die? The Bible doesn't say, so we try to find the answer by reading between the lines."

"Grandma, excuse me for interrupting," said Desy, "but you said to ask when I don't understand."

"That's right, Desy. Never hesitate to ask. We are here to learn. What's your question?"

"What do you mean 'read between the lines'? What is written between the lines?"

"Nothing."

"Nothing? How can you read something when there's nothing there?"

"Yeah, how can you read nothing?" Jade wondered. "If there's nothing, there's nothing. It seems weird to me, Grandma, that you can read something between the lines when there is nothing between the lines to read! Anyhow, how can you know that what you are reading is right?"

"Jade, I don't think we can be absolutely sure that what one is 'reading' is exactly what the writer intended to say. However, when we feel the writer left out something that he might have included to help us understand a situation, we fill in what we think he could have thought or written but didn't. For example, all of you would like an explanation for why God didn't make Cain die. Right?"

"Yes!" they quickly responded.

"But," Grandma continued, "the writer doesn't tell us. This is when we fill in to come up with a logical explanation. Do you want to know what *I* read in between the lines?"

"Yes, tell us!" the children said.

"Because Cain was very frightened and worried about what God might do to him, he lied to God. But when he finally got the courage to admit the truth, he fell on his knees and told God how very sorry he was for what he had done, and between his sobs he pleaded, 'Please forgive me, God. I really never meant to kill my brother and had no idea at all that by hitting him, I would cause him to die. Honestly, I never intended to kill Abel.' God, who knows everything, knew that Cain was deeply grieved and that he sincerely repented for his crime. And that is why I believe God allowed Cain to live."

"It's a good thing Cain came clean; otherwise, I think God would have made him die," Loren remarked.

"Well, children, I told you what I read between the lines. Would any of you like to read what's in between the lines?"

"No thanks," Marie said. "I'll accept

what you 'read.'"

The rest of the children went along with Marie.

"Do you understand now what is meant by 'reading between the lines'?"

"I . . . I guess so," Desy replied slowly, not completely convinced.

"But Grandma, not everyone who 'reads between the lines' comes up with the same ideas," Loren commented.

"You're right. That's why we have many different interpretations. I just gave you my idea. Not everyone would agree with me."

"I'll accept your explanation," Loren said. "It seems logical."

"Me too," Marie added.

"Glad you feel that way. And now to continue where I left off. Where did I stop?"

"Where Cain was scared that people would kill him," Loren said.

"Thanks, Loren. In order to protect Cain from those who might want to kill him, God put a mark on him."

"What kind of mark was it?" Angela asked.

"No one knows."

"I think God likes to keep us guessing," Angela said.

"What do you mean He likes to keep us guessing?" Grandma asked.

"Well," Angela replied, "He doesn't tell us what kind of fruit Adam and Eve ate. And now we don't know what kind of mark He put on Cain."

"Maybe He wants us to 'read between the lines,'" Desy said seriously. "Maybe He put a big star."

"No, Desy, it couldn't be a star. My teacher puts a star on my paper when I do good work," Loren said.

"Maybe it was a big black spot or a big black circle," Jade said.

"How about a tattoo?" Loren suggested.

"No, Loren, it couldn't be a tattoo because the Bible says mark, not a tattoo," Marie corrected.

"I think we can agree that it was a big

black mark," Grandma said quickly. "Our next question is: Where do you think God put the mark?"

"I am going to guess that God put it on his chest—no, on his arm," said Angela.

"I don't think so," Loren said.

"Why not, Loren?" Grandma asked.

"Well, let's say it could get cold where Cain lived. And if he put on a sweater—"

"I don't think they had sweaters in those days," Marie interrupted.

"Maybe you're right. So, he puts on a robe or a shawl or whatever, to keep warm, and people wouldn't be able to see the mark. Then Cain would really be in danger of being killed."

"Good thinking, Loren. Any other ideas?" Grandma asked.

"Maybe God put it on his nose. Every-one could see that," Angela said seriously.

"But it couldn't be black. I'd make it a red ball like a clown has on his nose. You couldn't miss that!" Desy added.

"That really would be funny," Loren said, laughing. "People might not kill him, but they sure would die laughing. Cain would be the brunt of their jokes and teasing. The poor fellow would be better off dead! I think God must have put the mark on his forehead. Everybody could see that."

"Do you all agree with Loren?"

The children nodded.

"I think Cain got off pretty easy," Jade complained.

"No, he didn't," Loren said. "Just think, Cain had to live the rest of his life with that mark on his forehead. How would you like people staring at you and pointing at that mark? I don't think he got off easy, as you put it. I kinda feel sorry for the guy."

"Not me. I don't feel sorry for him one bit. And I think God put a mark on Cain so that he couldn't ever forget, not for a minute, what he did," Marie said sternly.

"And you think that wasn't harsh punishment?" Loren asked.

"It wasn't easy, but Cain deserved it. He had it coming. He sinned, didn't he?"

Jade looked puzzled.

Grandma asked her, "Jade, is there something you don't understand?"

"I was just thinking that today we learned about a third sin that was committed by Cain. And Marie told us the first sin was committed by Lucifer."

"Now I'm confused," Angela interrupted. "I thought the first sin was when Adam and Eve ate the fruit they weren't supposed to eat. How can we have two first sins?"

"It's true that Lucifer, the Fallen Angel, was the first to commit a sin, but the first human beings—the first people—in the world to sin were Adam and Eve, and that's why their sin is called the 'original sin,'" Grandma explained.

"Excuse me, Grandma, what do you mean 'original sin'? What kind of sin is it?" Desy asked.

"Loren, do you think you can explain the word 'original'?"

"Yes, I can. Original comes from the word 'origin,' which means the first, or the beginning—where it started."

"Good. So, the 'original sin' is the sin committed by Adam and Eve. And because they disobeyed God, we are all born with original sin."

"Why?" Desy asked. "*We* didn't eat the apple—I mean, that special fruit. Why should we be punished for something we didn't do?"

"That's right! Eve sinned, not us!" Loren said.

"And Adam too!" Marie cut in. "Why do you always want to blame only Eve?"

"Okay, okay," Loren said. "They *both* sinned. Now can I continue?"

"Loren, *may* I continue," Grandma corrected gently.

"I often make that mistake but know better. Let me start over again."

Grandma nodded encouragingly.

"Adam and Eve sinned, not us," Loren said. "You said God is a just God. He is fair. I don't think our being punished for something that we didn't do is fair."

"I gotta agree with Loren and Jade. It's

not fair," Desy said.

"I don't think it's right either," Marie added.

"I don't either," Angela chimed in.

"You are all missing the point," Grandma said. "You're not being punished because Adam and Eve ate the forbidden fruit. You're not held responsible for their sin. But you must guard against the weakness you inherited from Adam and Eve to sin. And this weakness can persuade you to do the wrong thing or make bad decisions."

"But Grandma, I'm worried about making good decisions. You said we inherited free will and we can choose the good or the bad, but how do we know what to do?" Desy asked with a concerned look in her big eyes.

"For some of us making good choices is

natural, while for others making bad ones comes easy," Marie said, looking straight at Loren.

"What do you mean by that?" Loren challenged.

"Children, let's talk a little about what the inheritance of free will and making good and bad choices mean," Grandma said. "Many believe that we inherited the strengths and weaknesses of Adam and Eve—that we have two powerful forces within us that guide us and tell us what to do. Let's pretend we have a handsome, strong angel dressed in gleaming white armor, and a second angel dressed in coal-black armor. Whenever we make a decision, we listen to the two voices inside of us.

" 'Listen to me,' the white angel pleads. 'Do as I tell you. Yes, it may be difficult not to watch your favorite TV program, but I strongly recommend you do your homework first—'

" 'Nah, don't listen to him,' interrupts the black angel. 'He is such a party pooper. You need a break. You worked all day in school and ran some errands for your mom after you got home from school. You need to relax. You know the old saying, 'All work and no play makes for a dull day.' So go ahead, enjoy yourself. You can do your homework later. You'll have plenty of time to do both.'

" 'No, you won't,' objects the white angel. 'This TV program is too long, and you won't be able to get your work done.'

" 'Listen to that pessimist! You'll get it done, believe me.'

" 'Don't be persuaded by the black angel. He's bad news. He enjoys giving bad advice and getting people in trouble."

" 'Hey white angel, knock it off!' And the argument gets louder and louder," Grandma said. "Finally, we have to make a decision. What is our decision? To be influenced by the white angel or the black angel? Because of the 'original sin' we inherited, we have a tendency to do wrong things. But because God gave us the gift of free will, we can choose to be good or bad. We can decide to do the right thing or the wrong thing, and we can say yes or no to what is asked of us. The decision is up to us!"

"I would do my homework first," Marie said.

"Me too," Jade and Angela said in unison.

"I'm not so sure," Loren said.

"Loren!" all the girls shrieked.

"Just kidding," Loren grinned.

"So you see, Desy, to make good choices, look inside of yourself and you'll know what to do. God sends his angels to help when you ask. Oh dear, I don't know whether I explained it well. At least, I hope you understand 'original sin' a little better now. It is difficult to understand it fully."

"Oh Grandma, you don't have to explain it anymore. I understood it all," Marie said with a toss of her head.

"I'm glad you did, Marie. And you, Loren?"

"It was never explained to me before. I have to think about it, but you did give me a new interpretation of the 'original sin' that makes sense."

"And you, Jade?"

"I heard what you said, and I think I

understood most of it, but Grandma, I still think in a way it was a punishment and we are getting some of that punishment. Is it wrong for me not to agree completely with you? Oh, you know, I just can't help feeling that it's not fair."

"That's all right, Jade. There are people called biblical scholars who have studied the Bible most of their lives. They think they can explain what the Bible says or doesn't say, but even they don't always agree. So, take your time, think it over, and I'm sure you will come up with an answer that you will be comfortable with. And you, Desy?"

"Grandma, I would like you to go over it again."

"Oh no, Desy, not again!" Marie complained. "I'll explain it to you at home, I promise."

Desy accepted Marie's offer.

"And now let's hear from our youngest listener. Angela, did you understand my explanation?"

"Well, Grandma, I know Adam and Eve disobeyed God," Angela said. "I know we don't live in the Garden of Eden because we inherited something else. And it's a mystery why they blew it in the first place. You know my friend Paula, the one who lives next door to us?"

Grandma nodded.

"Well, she doesn't go to our church, but sometimes we talk about God. She said her priest—no, her minister and her Sunday school teacher—tell them that when they can't understand something. . . No, maybe I got that wrong. . . . When they can't understand what the Bible says, they still must believe just the same and not worry about it because it's a mystery. So, I'm going to do like she does, Grandma. I really didn't understand everything today. Neither did Chompers. Right, Chompers?"

Her faithful dog barked in agreement.

"How could Chompers know?" Marie asked scornfully. "You know, Angie, you shouldn't talk to Paula about God."

"Why not? She's my best friend. And she knows a lot about God and the Bible and—"

"That's what worries me. You haven't started going to religion classes yet, and she's been going ever since she was a baby."

"Since she was a baby! I don't believe that."

"I was exaggerating. Everybody knows Protestant parents send their kids to study their religion as early as possible."

"I don't see anything wrong with that. I still don't know what you're getting at," Loren said.

"I'm trying to warn Angela that Paula might convince her to go to her church."

"Oh, I've gone with Paula several times, and I enjoyed what her Sunday school teacher talked about, and the songs the kids sang. And everyone was so friendly and welcomed me and invited me to join them in their games. I like going with Paula to her Sunday school class."

"See, Grandma, why I'm warning Angela not to discuss religion with Paula and not to go to Paula's church?" Marie said.

"I still don't know why—"

"Angela, Paula is not Catholic! And she . . . well, she doesn't believe what we believe."

"There's nothing wrong with that."

"But Loren, Paula's not *Catholic*!" Marie repeated stubbornly.

"So what? You're just as narrow-minded as that kid in my class who wanted to start his own baseball club and invited everyone but me. Why? Because I'm Catholic."

"What a stupid kid!" Marie burst out angrily.

"And you're not doing the same thing?"

'Loren, you're not suggesting I'm as stupid as that kid?"

"I'm not *suggesting*, dear cousin; I'm telling you straight out. You shouldn't talk against anyone's religion."

"I'm not talking against anyone's religion. I'm only trying to warn Angela not to go to Paula's church because our church is the right one. Grandma, which church is the right one? Ours, of course." Marie answered her own question.

"Marie, we believe our church is the first Christian church and the right one, but many do not agree with us. We must respect everyone's beliefs and traditions. When I was a little girl and saw for the first time an American Indian medicine man singing, dancing, and shaking his rattlers, while other Indians were beating their drums, I thought it was funny and weird. Later on, I understood what all that singing and dancing meant. That medicine man was praying to God in the way he was taught. He was praying to God for his people and for himself. Now, do you think God accepted his prayers?"

"Yes," Loren answered quickly. "Because God is good. God is love. And since He is omniscient, God knew the medicine man was praying to Him."

"You said it all, Loren. God's love is the greatest gift to the world. And God looked into the medicine man's heart and saw his love and desire to serve the Great Spirit—the Indians' name for God—the way he knew how. And since we're talking about people's religion, let me ask you: what was Jesus' religion?"

"Catholic, of course," Marie answered with conviction.

"Loren?"

"I don't know. I never thought about it. Marie seems so sure of her answer. Maybe I should go along with her."

"You're playing it safe, Loren," Marie said. "I know I'm right."

"Jade?"

"I'm not sure."

"And you, Desy?"

"I know my sister is very smart, so I guess I'll say Catholic."

"Angela, may we have your answer now?"

"Could he maybe be a—a—*Protestant*?"

"No way! Impossible! Did Paula tell you that?" Marie burst out angrily.

"No, we never talked about Jesus' religion," Angela said. "Who has the right answer, Grandma?"

"No one. Jesus didn't have a religion!" Loren interjected.

"Oh yes, he surely did. Jesus was Jewish," Grandma replied.

"What? Jewish!"

"He certainly was. He was born a Jew, grew up a Jew, and He died a Jew."

"Well I'll be!" Loren exclaimed. "I would have never guessed it. Then how come we're Catholics?" he asked. "And why are there Protestants and all the other religions? How come we're not all Jewish?"

"It's a long story, but as we continue to study the Bible, we'll learn why we're not all Jewish, and we should thank the Jewish people for teaching us about God and preparing us for the coming of Jesus. We have much in common with our Jewish brothers and sisters, and we owe them a lot. Now let's get back to Cain."

The children were curious to know what happened to Cain after he had been marked. Grandma told them that Cain left his parents and went to the land of Nod. "He finally got married and had a family, and—"

"Just a minute, Grandma," Marie interrupted. "Did you say Cain got married?"

Grandma nodded.

"Who did he marry?"

"*Whom* did he marry?" Grandma corrected gently.

"Okay, okay, Grandma. *Whom* did he marry? And another thing, Grandma: you said that Cain was scared the people would kill him. Who are these people? I've been thinking pretty hard and—"

"I thought I smelled smoke," Loren said teasingly.

"Oh, shut up, and—"

"No, no, Marie," Grandma said, shaking her index finger.

"Sorry, Grandma, but he makes me so mad."

"I meant to say that it must be difficult for you to think hard." Loren continued teasing Marie.

"All right, smarty-pants, maybe you can explain. Go ahead. I want to hear your brilliant explanation."

"I don't have to explain. The answer is simple. Just accept what the Bible says."

"And what does the Bible say?"

"Oh, we're not going to go over that again. Just accept and stop arguing."

"Loren, I think we owe Marie the courtesy of letting her finish her question," Grandma said.

"Thanks, Grandma. I'd like to know what people Cain is talking about. I thought there were only four people on earth: Adam, Eve, Cain, and Abel. So, who are these people? And where did they come from? And where did Cain find a wife? And who—I mean whom—did he marry?"

"Very good questions. I wish I knew the answers."

"You don't know, Grandma?" Jade was surprised.

Grandma shook her head.

"Who *does* know the answers?"

Grandma shrugged and shook her head again. She was quiet for a minute or two. Then she said softly, "Would you like to hear what some biblical scholars have to say? I think their explanation is worth knowing, although not everyone agrees."

"I would like to hear it," Marie said eagerly.

"Me, too," Loren added. "I'd like to hear it even though I might end up disagreeing."

"How about you younger ones? Would you like me to explain how they understood this part of the Bible?"

All three nodded.

"Okay," Grandma began. "Some people believe that Cain and Abel were teenagers when Cain killed his brother. Others believe that this sad incident happened many years later, maybe a hundred years or more. They also believe—and the Bible says so—that Adam and Eve had many children. At the beginning, brothers and sisters married one another. As the years went by, families grew larger and larger, and pretty soon there were a lot of people.

"And now, Marie, let's see if we can find answers to your questions. Who are the people that Cain feared might kill him? The children, grandchildren, great-grandchildren, great-great-children, and so on, of Adam and Eve. Some people believe that these are the people that Cain is worried about. Now, where did he find a wife? From his own people. Whom did he marry? He must have married a great-great-great—who knows how many greats—niece or cousin."

"Excuse me, Grandma, are you saying that Cain got married when he was a hundred years old?" Desy asked in disbelief.

"Oh, Desy, how could he get married so old?" Jade said. "Why, he'd be older than my grandfather. Too old to get married. I don't believe that's the right explanation. I can't go along with it, Grandma."

"I can't either," Loren added.

"After he got married, did he finally settle down in one place?"

"He and his wife moved away. He built a new city and named it Enoch after his first son."

The children felt sorry for Adam and Eve for having lost their son Abel and now Cain, who moved far away, but Grandma assured them that although that was sad, "Adam and Eve had other children. Adam and Eve lived a long time."

"How long did God allow Adam and Eve to live?" Loren asked.

"Adam lived to be nine hundred and thirty years old," Grandma replied.

"Nine hundred and thirty years!" Marie and Loren exclaimed in unison.

Loren and Marie were very good at arithmetic and this number made an impression on them. It was unbelievable! Surely Grandma must have misread the Bible.

"Is that a long time?" Desy asked. The younger ones couldn't imagine what nine hundred really meant.

"It's like forever!" Marie exclaimed. "Grandma, are you sure that Adam and Eve lived that long? Maybe you don't remember. When people get old—not that you're old—what I'm trying to say is . . . is . . ."

Loren came to his cousin's rescue: "I think what Marie is trying to say is that it's hard to believe that anyone could live that long."

Marie gave him a grateful look.

"Grandma, do you really believe that Adam lived to be . . . how old did you say?" Jade asked.

"Nine hundred and thirty years."

"Does the Bible really say that?"

"Yes, Jade, the Bible really says that. Do I believe it? Should I question the Bible?"

"I heard my papa tell my mamma that he doesn't believe everything he reads in the newspaper."

"I agree with your father, Desy, but the Bible is not a newspaper. Remember, the Bible is divinely inspired. The newspaper, heaven knows, is not. Some Bible experts aren't sure if the people of those days counted years differently from the way we do, or if people really lived that long."

"Did Adam live the longest?" Angela wanted to know.

"No, Methuselah did. He lived to be nine hundred and sixty-nine years old."

"Nine hundred and sixty-nine years

old! That's almost a thousand years. I just can't believe that, even if it says so in the Bible," Marie said.

"Maybe you should rewrite the Bible," Loren teased. "But wait until you're inspired."

"Oh, you're so funny. You can't be that dumb to believe anyone can live almost a thousand years. You really don't believe that, do you?"

Loren hesitated.

"Go ahead, Mr. Know-It-All, answer yes or no."

"Yes or no," Loren said seriously.

"And what is that supposed to mean? You're so stupid, you can't even make up your mind one way or the other," Marie said harshly.

"Not as stupid as you are. Grandma said the Bible is divinely inspired but written by people. Maybe the person may have written what he thought God wanted him to write, or . . ." Loren turned to Grandma for help.

"I think you are on the right track, Loren, and I don't blame Marie for thinking that no one can live that long. May I make a suggestion? Why don't we accept what is written until someone comes up with a better explanation. Okay?"

They all nodded.

"And how long did Eve live?" Marie wanted to know.

"The Bible doesn't say. It only mentions the ages of men."

"I'm disappointed. Why doesn't the Bible tell us Eve's age at her death?" Marie said.

"Because the Bible writers were smart and they knew that women try to hide their age. And, as I tried to tell you, Adam is more important than Eve," Loren said with a smirk.

"Oh you . . . you give me a pain in the—" Marie's cheeks were red with frustration.

"Shall we continue?" Grandma interrupted.

"Grandma, who was Methuselah?" Jade asked.

"He was Noah's grandfather."

"You mean Noah, the one who built a boat and put a lot of animals on it?"

"Yes, he's the one. Well, children, I think we've had enough Bible for today. Let's go outside and breathe some fresh air."

"Grandma, don't you think we should first go over what we learned today?" Marie asked.

"I thought perhaps you all needed a break. Today's lesson might have been a little . . . perhaps not difficult, but maybe not easy either."

"Oh, not for me, Grandma. I understood it very well."

"Glad to hear that. But for the others, a little fresh air might be good for them."

"Grandma, I hate to be a nuisance, but I really think we should have a review — even a short one," Marie insisted.

"Marie, I must tell you how much I admire you for having the courage to admit that you are a nuisance," Loren said in an exaggerated, awestruck voice.

"Grandma, don't be surprised if one of these days I bop Loren on the head."

"Oh dear, I hope it doesn't come to that. All right, Marie, let's have the review. Would you like to start it?"

"Glad to. Cain and Abel were the first two sons of Adam and Eve. Cain offered a gift to God, but God wouldn't accept it, though God did accept Abel's gift. Cain blamed Abel for God's refusal and killed his brother."

"Good. Next, Loren?"

"Even though Cain lied to God, God is omniscient and knew everything that had happened, so of course He had to punish Cain. God put a mark on Cain in order to protect him and prevent him from being killed. Cain became a hobo."

"Jade?"

"Then you explained what 'Am I my brother's keeper?' means. And now we know we must take care of one another because we are all God's children."

"Desy, I believe you are next."

"Then you explained what 'original sin' means. It's a little difficult so I won't try explaining it, if that's all right with you, Grandma."

"That's okay, Desy. And now for you, Angela."

"Well, Grandma, I understood some of the lesson. I remember Adam lived a long time. I can't remember exactly how long . . ."

"Nine hundred and thirty years," Marie said.

"Thanks, Marie, but the one who lived the longest . . . I can't remember his name either"

"Methuselah," Loren offered.

"I think you said he was Noah's grand-father. And tomorrow you are going to tell us about Noah and all the animals. I know I'm going to like that story."

Angela turned to Chompers and said sweetly, "Oh Chompers, you're going to like the story of Noah too, because it has lots of animals in it." Chompers lovingly licked Angela on the cheek, as she put her arms around the dog.

Princess felt she had been ignored, and she was jealous that Chompers always got affectionate hugs from Angela. She purred softly and rubbed her head against Loren's knees. Loren got the message. He picked Princess up and patted her affectionately.

"Sorry, Princess," he said, "I didn't mean to neglect you. I was concentrating on what Grandma was saying."

Princess purred even louder, happy to be in Loren's arms.

"And now let's go look at my pretty flowers," Grandma said.

"Grandma, one more thing before we go out," Marie said. "We almost forgot about the three sins."

"Oh no, I thought this was supposed to be a *short* review," Loren moaned.

"Loren, it's important to know about the three sins." Before Grandma could stop her, Marie began: "Lucifer committed the first sin. He wanted to be more powerful than God, but he lost out and was kicked out of Heaven and thrown way down to Hell. Adam and Eve committed the 'original sin' when they ate the forbidden fruit. They were banished from the Garden of Eden and had to enter an imperfect world. The third sin was committed by Cain when he killed his brother, Abel. Cain had to give up a life of ease for a life of hardship."

"That's fine, Marie."

"Thank you, Grandma."

"May I add one thing?" Loren requested.

"Of course," Grandma said.

"We learned from all this that if you sin, you have to pay a price—you have to pay the consequence."

"Correct, Loren. When we sin, we have to face the consequences of what we've done."

"I just thought it was important to review about the sins," Marie said.

"Very good idea, Marie. You said it well. I think that finishes our lesson for today."

As they walked toward the door, Grandma could hear them discussing some of their reactions to what they had learned.

Marie was still angry. "Loren, you got to admit that Cain did a terrible thing."

"I'm not denying that."

"Yes, he was bad," Desy agreed.

"And if you're bad, you go to Hell. It's as simple as that. If you're good, you go to Heaven; if you're bad, you go to Hell."

"Not always," Loren argued. "There are times when you repent and . . ."

Finally, the voices faded away as the children reached the garden. Angela returned and poked her head in the door and yelled, "Sorry, Gabby. I didn't talk to you today, but I promise to talk to you tomorrow! Be a good bird, Gabby! Goodbye!"

"Gabby, good bird! Goodbye!"

About the Author

Laura Lipari has a lot of stories to tell in addition to her wonderful children's stories. The 102-year-old author is a retired high school teacher of Italian and French, and served as an adjunct college professor of Spanish.

Raised in Ohio, she met her husband while studying in Italy, where they lived for eight years. While they were there, World War II broke out. Because of her superb linguistic skills, she was invited to serve as an interpreter for the US Army's intelligence wing. She is credited with saving hundreds of lives because of her service. She has many war stories to tell, including escaping on horseback from Nazi troops invading Italy. But writing about her faith is her first love.

Laura earned her Bachelor of Arts degree at Case Western Reserve University in Cleveland and attended the University of Perugia near Rome, Italy. She worked toward her master's degree at Perugia and at the University of Mexico.

Laura has five children, nine grandchildren, and six great-grandchildren.

As may be seen in her writing, Laura has a wonderful sense of humor. She told her publisher: "I hope this is the beginning of a long relationship. I have several more books in the works!"

About the Illustrator

Nancy Ladd is a devout Christian who combines her love of scientific research with a trained artistic eye. Nancy sees her experiences as a mother, wife, grandmother, and great-grandmother as opportunities to share her gifts with others.

When she is not helping her family and doing professional art projects, she collects, researches, and documents stories about her family, which have been passed down orally through the generations.

Nancy attended Immaculate Heart College, the Art Center School, and earned her BA at the University of Arizona, majoring in art.

REDSCORPION PRESS

Red Scorpion Press was formed in January 2016 with the hope of bettering the world in a small way through publishing. Our aim is to push boundaries and be an outlet for fresh voices and unique perspectives that entertain and inform.

Please visit us at www.redscorpionpress.com for our latest selection of books.